*Happy Snow Days! Joshua E Judge*

# BE NICE TO THE WEATHER GUY

# A New England Christmas Story

By Josh Judge

Illustrated by Ginger Nielson

Peter E. Randall Publisher

2017

This book is dedicated to the boys and girls of CHaD. You are all the greatest.

Also to the men and women who work to improve the lives of these children, thank you.

That's why 100% of the profits from this book are being donated to CHaD.

CHaD®

Children's Hospital at Dartmouth-Hitchcock

*www.chadkids.org*

’Twas the night before Christmas
and all through the station,
news anchors reported the latest taxation.

The sportscasters cheered as the Patriots won.

And the weather folks promised we'd see lots of sun.

The viewers were watching all snug in their bed,
they watched 'cause their TV remotes had gone dead,
which forced them to hear all the things that I said.

I spoke of bare ground as I forecast ahead.

I looked at my maps, then I looked a bit more,
yet I only saw rainstorms and warm temps in store.
When what to my wondering eyes should appear,
but a miniature snowstorm, that was getting quite near!

I leapt from my news desk, it caused such a clatter,
I ran to the window, even climbed up a ladder,
when off in the distance I thought I could see,
an approaching Nor'easter?!? Could it really be?

From the top of the ladder, to the top of the station,
I climbed every building and tower in frustration!

Then atop Mt. Washington
viewers heard me exclaim,
a phrase that made children and
adults just the same,
go into a frenzy of joy and delight,
while I Twittered and Facebooked
and yelled from high height:

"Here comes our snowstorm; I've got it in sight!
Merry Christmas to all, and to all a good night!"

And the folks of New Hampshire,
Massachusetts, and Maine,

woke up the next morning and called me...
VERY BAD NAMES!

For you see, it DID snow, and it snowed all night long,
but it snowed much too fast and it snowed
much too strong!
In fact, there was so much of the white stuff you see,
that the snowbanks were higher than a large
maple tree!

The cars were all buried, the roads out of sight,
and the snow was quite heavy, not fluffy and light.
Try as we did, and we tried that whole day,
there was nowhere to put all that snow
in our way.

Well I shoveled and plowed and worked with my spouse,
so that family and friends could come to our house,

and under the piles,
snowbanks, and drifts,
I found a sad sight;
were they all frozen stiff?

For you see, under all those mountains of snow,
was a poor jolly old chap, who'd been trapped on the go.
And it wasn't just him that had lost all his cheer,
there was also a sleigh and eight tiny reindeer.

We dug them all out and they went on their way.
They thanked us for digging, and, though it's cliché,
they said "Merry Christmas to all" in a hurry,
then took off so fast it made our eyes blurry!

So the lesson in all of this holiday snow,
a moral to share when the winds start to blow:
Be careful what you wish for,
enjoy the status quo,
and be nice to the weather guy
or you'll get too much snow!

# WEATHER FACTS

**Could the events in this book really happen?**
While snow storms DO sometimes surprise even
meteorologists, it isn't possible for THAT much snow to fall
in just a few hours. Around here, they get the MOST snow on
top of Mount Washington.

**The highest amount of snow ever recorded** at Mount
Washington's summit in 24-hours was 49.3" (in 1969).

**Biggest single snow storms EVER for select cities:**
- Concord, NH - 27.5" (March 11, 1888)
- Boston, MA -27.5" (Feb. 18–19, 2003)
- Portland, ME - 24.4" (Jan. 17–18, 1979)

**What's the most snow those cities ever got in a whole
winter?**
- Concord, NH - 122" (Winter of 1873–74)
- Boston, MA - 110.6" (Winter of 2014–15)
- Portland, ME - 107.6" (Winter of 1970–71)

**Snow is very important.** It melts into water for lakes,
streams, and for your house.

A "Nor'easter" is a storm that sometimes brings a LOT of snow, and yes, the wind blows from the northeast. Believe it or not, they can be either snow OR rain!

**You know what snow is, but what is the difference between SLEET and FREEZING RAIN?**

**SLEET:** Rain that freezes into ice as it is falling through the air. It lands as ice pellets.

**FREEZING RAIN:** When it is raining and it is so cold out that the rain instantly freezes into ice when it hits the cold ground.

**What is a blizzard?** That's when the wind blows snow around strong enough to make it so you can't see very far in front of you.

**The largest snowman ever made was 122 feet tall!**
It was built in Bethel, Maine, in 2008. It took over a month to build and hundreds of people helped. It was only a few feet shorter than the Statue of Liberty!
The buttons were made of truck tires and the arms were entire trees!

*This book wouldn't have been possible without the amazing support, help, and ideas from my wife, Diane. Also, the incredible illustration talents of Ginger Nielson are what made these pages so fantastic.*

*Thank you so much to both of you.*

Published by Peter E. Randall Publisher

ISBN-13: 9781937721466
Library of Congress Control Number: 2017944934

Printed in the United States of America